Books should be returned on or before the last date stamped below.

2 2 MAY 2006

0 2 APR 2007   2 2 MAR 2011

1 9 AUG 2008

1 2 MAY 2009   2 9 APR 2015

21. APR 10.

1 2 APR 2011

-3 MAY 2016

-6 APR 2018

- 4 MAY 2011

-6 DEC 2011

WITHDRAWN FROM LIBRARY

ABERDEENSHIRE LIBRARIES

WITHDRAWN FROM LIBRARY

ABERDEENSHIRE LIBRARIES

**ABERDEENSHIRE LIBRARY
AND INFORMATION SERVICE
MELDRUM MEG WAY, OLDMELDRUM**

Rock, Lois

Rock, Lois

WITHDRAWN FROM LIBRARY

ABERDEENSHIRE LIBRARIES

J745.
5

1680635

D1550011

A L I S

1680635

FIRST FESTIVALS

Easter

Lois Rock

LION
Children's Books

Introduction

Text and artefacts by Lois Rock
Illustrations copyright © 1999 Helen Cann
Photography by John Williams Studios, Thame
This edition copyright © 2003 Lion Publishing

The moral rights of the author and illustrator
have been asserted

Published by
Lion Publishing plc
Mayfield House, 256 Banbury Road
Oxford OX2 7DH, England
www.lion-publishing.co.uk
ISBN 0 7459 4653 4

First hardback edition 1999
First paperback edition 2003
10 9 8 7 6 5 4 3 2 1

All rights reserved

A catalogue record for this book is
available from the British Library

Typeset in 18/21 Baskerville MT Schlbk
Printed and bound in China

Acknowledgments
The stories in this book are retold from the Bible.

Bible references

6 A Story for Lent: Matthew chapter 4.

7 Stories of Jesus: Luke chapter 12, 19.

10 Palm Sunday: Matthew chapter 21;
Mark chapter 11; Luke chapter 19;
John chapter 12.

11 Good Friday: Matthew chapters 26–27;
Mark chapters 14–15; Luke chapters 22–23;
John chapters 13–19.

12 A Green Hill: Matthew chapters 27–28;
Mark chapter 15; Luke chapters 23–24;
John chapter 19.

13 Easter Sunday: Matthew chapter 28;
Mark chapter 16; Luke chapter 24;
John chapter 20.

ABERDEENSHIRE LIBRARY AND INFORMATION SERVICE	
1680635	
CAW	342407
J745.5	£5.99
SC	NFPS

This book is one of a series dealing with the Christian festivals.

This one is about the special days leading up to Easter.

Here are traditional crafts and foods, along with simple instructions that children and grown-ups can follow together.

Here are the Bible stories that have shaped the season and its celebrations.

Here is a book to deepen a child's understanding of the Christian heritage.

Contents

1 Pancake Day

2 Making Pancakes

3 Mardi Gras

4 Carnival Mask

5 Lent

6 A Story for Lent

7 Stories of Jesus

8 Mothering Sunday

9 A Posy of Flowers

10 Palm Sunday

11 Good Friday

12 A Green Hill

13 Easter Sunday

14 Trees at Easter

15 Flowers and Birds

16 Easter Poem

17 Easter Nest

18 Easter Bunnies

19 Easter Basket

20 Easter Card

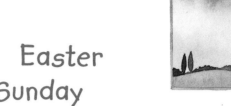

Pancake Day

In the middle of winter, spring seems far away. It will be a long wait till Easter. A party will cheer everyone up!

Seven weeks before Easter comes a special party Tuesday. One tradition is to have a pancake party.

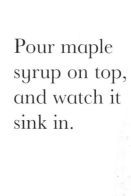

Enjoy your pancakes with lots of different fillings.

Some people like to roll their pancakes. Some fold them. How do you like to eat your pancakes?

Pour maple syrup on top, and watch it sink in.

Sprinkle caster sugar on the pancake. Add a squeeze of juice from a lemon wedge.

Spread your pancake with jam… and cream too!

Pancake games

Put a cooked pancake in a cool frying-pan. Try tossing it and catching it the other side up!

How many times can you toss and turn it in a minute?

Try tossing and turning the pancake as you run along. Who can run the fastest race and still keep their pancake? (It's best to play this game outside, in case you drop the pancake!)

Making Pancakes

Here's how to make pancakes that are sweet and delicious. The pancakes are quite thick, which makes them easy to lift and turn. They also last quite well if you play tossing games with them!

You will need

300 g self-raising flour

75 g caster sugar

25 g butter or margarine

1 tbsp golden syrup

500 ml milk

2 eggs

mixing bowl

mixing spoon

small glass bowl

glass tumbler

cooking oil

frying-pan

kitchen towel

ladle

spatula

big casserole dish

1 Put the flour in the mixing bowl. Add the sugar. Stir to make a big hole in the middle of the flour and sugar mix.

2 Put the butter or margarine in a glass bowl. Add the syrup and 100 ml milk. Microwave on full for 2 minutes. Pour into the hole in the flour.

6 Add extra milk as you stir. Keep adding more and stirring until the mixture is like thick cream.

7 Pour a spoonful of oil into the frying-pan. Wipe the oil all over the inside of the pan with a piece of kitchen towel.

☺ *Ask a grown-up to help you cook.*

☺ *Always wash your hands before you begin.*

3 Break the eggs one by one into the tumbler.

4 Add the eggs to the mixture in the large bowl.

5 Stir the liquid in small circles, then stir wider to mix in the flour and sugar.

8 Heat the pan on the stove. After about 2 minutes, or when you think the pan is hot, lift the pan off the stove and add one ladleful of pancake mix.

9 Let the pancake cook for about a minute. Then take it off the heat so you can try lifting it with a spatula. When it is light brown on the underside, flip it over. Put the pan back on the heat to cook the other side.

10 Make more pancakes in the same way. Stack them in a big casserole dish and keep them warm until you are ready to eat them.

3 Mardi Gras

In some places, people have a carnival on party Tuesday. They call it the *Mardi Gras* festival. At the carnival, people wear amazing costumes. Everyone enjoys seeing the costumes in a big parade, and then they enjoy a party together.

Mardi is a French word. It means Tuesday. *Gras* is another French word, and it means 'fat'. People often eat a lot of fattening foods on the *Mardi Gras* festival. They plan to live more simply in the seven weeks till Easter.

Shrove Tuesday

This day is also called Shrove Tuesday. Shrove is a very old word which people hardly use any more. It means 'forgiven'. There is a tradition among Christians of going to church to say sorry to God for doing wrong things, and of remembering their belief that God forgives them.

These splendid costumes are simply bright T-shirts and tights, worn with a mask and frills. Find out how to make the mask and frills on the next page.

4 Carnival Mask

The spectacular bird mask is just a big roll of card with eyeholes, which you decorate with a beak and feather design.

Add a frill to cover the gap between the bottom of the mask and the top of the T-shirt.

Make more frills to wear on your arms and legs.

You will need

coloured card 35 cm x 60 cm

strong adhesive tape

chalk

cutting board and craft knife

smaller pieces of card in different colours

scissors

glue and brush

pencil and ruler

crêpe paper

stapler

beak

Copy these shapes to decorate your mask, or make up your own designs.

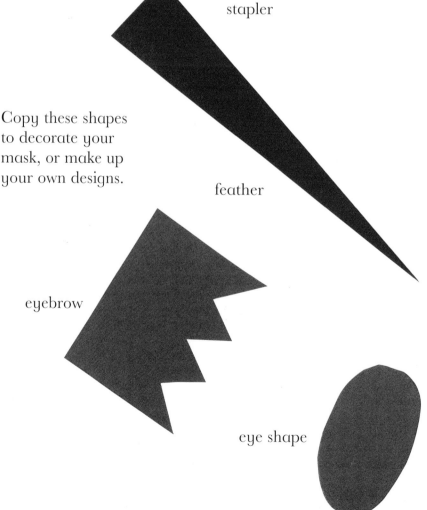

feather

eyebrow

eye shape

1 Curl your card round your head and lightly tape it into a cylinder, with the join at the back. On the outside mark with chalk where your eyes and nose are.

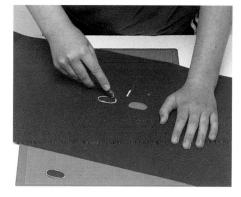

2 Lay the card flat on the cutting mat. Chalk in an oval shape for the eyes. Cut out the eyeholes carefully with a craft knife.

3 On smaller pieces of card, draw shapes like the ones shown here for beak, eyebrows and feathers. Cut them out with scissors.

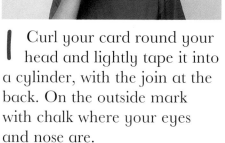

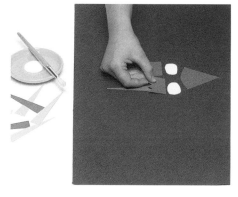

4 Glue these pieces in place to make a face.

5 Cut strips of card 2.5 cm wide and long enough to fit round the bottom of the mask. Mark lines at 3 cm intervals.

6 Work out how deep you want your frill to be. Cut a piece from a roll of crêpe paper this deep. Now make a zigzag fold between each set of lines on the card strip to pleat the crêpe paper. Staple each pleat in place.

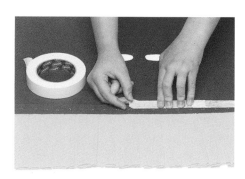

7 Tape the pleated strip on to the wrong side of the flat mask. Now you can recurl the mask around your head and tape it into a cylinder on the inside.

8 Make leg and arm frills in the same way. Cut a second length of card for each frill and glue it on to the back of the first one to cover the staples. Simply tape each frill in place around your arms or legs.

5 Lent

The seven weeks between party time on Shrove Tuesday and Easter are the season called Lent. It is wintertime. The trees are bare. You can see through the tracery of branches to the clear winter sky.

The Christian tradition of Lent is to spend time looking beyond everyday things—to think about God and the things that are really good and lovely and valuable.

Ash Wednesday

In the Christian year, the day after party Tuesday is known as Ash Wednesday. In some churches, people gather for a special service to say goodbye to all the bad things of the year gone by. The priest brings a small bowl of ashes—which are a symbol of old things being gone for ever—and smudges a little ash on the forehead of those that wish.

6 A Story for Lent

The story of Lent is part of the story of Jesus. It tells of Jesus going out into the wilderness. There, he spent many days thinking about what he must do in order to live as God wanted.

Long ago, in a hot, dry land called Palestine, lived a man named Jesus. In the little town of Nazareth, people knew him as the son of Joseph the carpenter. Yet his mother, Mary, remembered that an angel had foretold his birth, and said that her baby was God's own Son.

Now Jesus was grown up. He had learned the story of his own people, the Jews. He knew the writings that told of things that had happened in days gone by, and of the God in whom they believed. And now Jesus felt he was being called to tell his people more about God, and to show them such love that they would see what God's love must be like.

So it was that Jesus went off by himself into the brown and dusty wilderness. In the day lizards scuttled under stones, and eagles circled overhead; in the night, the eyes of wild animals glowed in the moonlight… foxes, wolves, bears… maybe a lion.

There, Jesus spent forty days, wondering about what lay ahead. He thought of nothing else. He did not even eat. Then, when he was very hungry, it seemed to him that the one his people called Satan, the one who tried to lead people away from God, came and spoke to him.

'If you are God's Son,' whispered Satan, 'order this stone to turn into bread.'

'No,' replied Jesus. 'For it is written, "People do not live on bread alone."'

So Satan led Jesus to think of all the kingdoms in the world. 'I will give you all this,' he whispered, 'power and riches. Worship me, and they will be yours.'

'No,' replied Jesus. 'For it is written, "Worship the Lord your God; serve God alone."'

So Satan led Jesus to think of Jerusalem, the great city of their people, and the golden temple where they worshipped God. 'If you are God's Son,' he whispered, 'you could throw yourself down from the highest point of the Temple. For it is written, "God will order the angels to take care of you, so you will not even hurt your feet on the stones."'

'No,' replied Jesus, 'For it is written, "You must not put God to the test."'

Then Satan went away. Jesus went back to where he lived, and began his work of telling people about God.

7 Stories of Jesus

These two stories give a glimpse of Jesus at work telling people about God and how to live as God wants.

Don't be greedy

'Watch out that you are not greedy,' said Jesus. 'Having lots of things does not make your life important… not even if you are very rich.

'Listen to this story: there was once a man whose farm gave him wonderful harvests. But he had a big problem: "Where can I store my crops?" he worried. "I know: I'll tear down my barns and build bigger ones. There, I can keep everything I have safe. Then I can say to myself, 'Lucky man, you have all you need for years and years. Take life easy! Eat, drink and enjoy yourself.'"

'But God said to him, "Foolish man! Tonight is the night you die! Now who will have all the good things you have kept for yourself?"

'And that,' said Jesus, 'is how it is with some people. They are rich in the things they own, but they are not rich in the things that matter to God.

'Look at the birds: they do not sow seeds and harvest crops, yet God looks after them. You are worth more than the birds.

'And look at the wild flowers. They do not work or make clothes for themselves, yet God gives them clothes more beautiful than any that the world's richest king can buy. If God takes care of the flowers, don't you think that God will take care of you?

'So don't worry about money and the things you can buy. Instead, give what you have to the poor. Spend your lives doing what is important to God. Then you will be rich in God's eyes: rich for ever.'

Zacchaeus

One day, Jesus came to the town of Jericho. There lived a man named Zacchaeus. He collected taxes from the people… and everyone knew that he cheated, asking for more than was right. So it was that the crowds who gathered to see Jesus would not let Zacchaeus through—and because he was a very short man, he could not see anything.

So Zacchaeus climbed a tree and watched, out of sight.

When Jesus came along, he stopped right under the tree and looked up. 'Come down, Zacchaeus!' he called. 'I want to stay in your house today.'

The crowds began to grumble. 'Who is this Jesus?' they muttered. 'What's all this they say about him being from God? He has gone to the house of someone who is well known for doing wrong things.'

Something must have happened as Jesus and Zacchaeus talked, for at the end of the day Zacchaeus stood up and said: 'Listen, I am going to give half of what I own to the poor, and if I have cheated anyone, I will pay them back four times what I took.'

Jesus said, 'Today, someone has been rescued; salvation has come. My work is to bring God to those who were far away from God.'

8 Mothering Sunday

Into the seven weeks of Lent comes a special day: Mothering Sunday. In days gone by, it was a holiday when everyone tried to go to the church in which they had grown up and learned about Jesus. This was almost always close to the home where their parents lived, so it became a day for families to enjoy together.

Nowadays, Mothering Sunday has become a day when children try to visit their mother, and perhaps prepare a special treat for her!

Here is a gift to make for Mothering Sunday.

A flower vase

You will need

glass jar

gesso

paintbrush

acrylic paint

old saucer

piece of sponge

piece of scrap paper

(if you like) clear varnish

1 Paint the glass jar with gesso all over the outside. When the first coat is dry, add a second coat. Let that dry too.

2 Squeeze some acrylic paint onto the saucer. Dab the sponge in the paint and then onto a piece of scrap paper. Then dab the sponge on the jar to leave a pretty mark. Do this as many times as you need to cover the jar.

3 If you like, brush a band of colour around the top. Leave the paint to dry. You may wish to cover the jar with clear varnish to protect the paint.

You can make a posy of
flowers that will fit neatly
into your vase.

You will need

spring flowers

budding twigs

evergreen twigs

raffia

scissors

1 Choose flowers and twigs.
Arrange them in a posy.
If you are giving a jar vase as
well, make sure the posy fits
snugly in the vase. Trim the
stems to the same level.

2 Wind raffia round the
stems to hold them
together. The posy is ready
to give as a gift.

10 Palm Sunday

The Sunday before Easter is called Palm Sunday. Christians remember a special day in the life of Jesus.

For three years Jesus travelled the land of Palestine. He told stories. He taught people about God. He was a friend to the friendless. Even more marvellous, he could work miracles. With just a touch, he healed many who were sick.

Then, one year, came the time for a great religious festival at the Temple in Jerusalem. People travelled from far and wide to celebrate. Crowds were on the road to the city when the cry rang out: 'Jesus is coming! Jesus is coming!' And over the hill he came, riding a donkey.

Everyone was eager to see Jesus. Everyone had heard stories about him and the things he did. What might he do now? They waved and cheered as if Jesus were a great king. They threw their coats on the road, to make a carpet for his donkey to walk on. They cut branches from the palm trees in the fields by the road and waved them like banners. Surrounded by a waving, cheering crowd, Jesus rode into Jerusalem.

Palm Sunday Processions

Some Christians celebrate Palm Sunday with a procession. The palm leaves that people waved on that first procession day were fresh and green. But now people know what happened to Jesus next: how the cheering crowd turned against him, and had him put to death on a cross of wood. The palm leaves that people wave in processions today are ones that have been folded into a cross.

Palm cross

You will need

palm leaves or strips of green or brown paper

scissors

1 Take one strip of palm leaf and make three small folds as shown to create a little pocket.

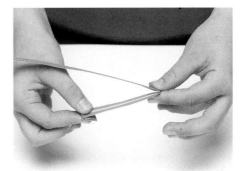

2 Hold the pocket tight against the leaf and make a backwards fold a few centimetres away. This is one half of the crosspiece.

3 Now work out where to fold the leaf for the other edge of the crosspiece, with enough over to fold back under the pocket. Snip the leaf at this point and hold the crosspiece in place.

4 Take a second strip of palm leaf and slip the blunt end into the under part of the pocket.

5 Hold the pocket so it does not slip and wind the long part of the leaf round the centre of the crosspiece. Tuck the pointed end through the pocket on top of the blunt end and gently pull through till it makes a tight 'knot'.

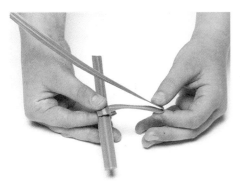

6 Slip the pointed end back through the upper part of the pocket and pull through.

7 Now fold the leaf down to make the top of the cross.

11 Good Friday

The week between Palm Sunday and Easter Sunday is sometimes called Holy Week. In that time, Jesus' enemies plotted to get rid of him.

Not everyone liked Jesus. Among his own people were those who hated him.

Some of the people who hated him were rabbis and priests. They spent their lives studying the writings of their people and teaching people what they said about God and how to live by the laws. They hated Jesus for the way he welcomed wrongdoers, and told them that God forgave them. 'How dare he speak like this?' they raged. 'What knowledge does Jesus have compared to us?'

While Jesus was in Jerusalem, those who hated him got together. They made secret plans to catch Jesus— alone.

On the very night of the festival itself, Jesus shared a meal with his friends. He gave them one last thing to remember:

'I am giving you a new commandment,' he said. 'Love one another, as I have loved you.'

But one of those friends was untrue. It was Judas. He slipped away to meet Jesus' enemies. For just thirty silver coins he told them where they could find Jesus.

That night, in the dark shade of an olive grove, Jesus sat awake, praying to God. Then came footsteps. Judas returned and greeted him in the usual way, with a kiss. Armed men sprang out from behind. They arrested Jesus and led him away.

Through the night, Jesus faced many questions. His enemies wanted to prove he had done something wrong, something terrible which would mean a terrible punishment.

They could find nothing against him, but they were cunning. They arranged for people to tell lies, claiming that Jesus was a dangerous rebel.

The next morning, they led Jesus to the governor of the land, Pontius Pilate.

'Are you wanting to be king?' Pilate asked Jesus. 'Are you wanting to get rid of me and those who rule the land?'

Pilate listened to Jesus' answers. 'I find nothing wrong with this man,' he said. 'I think I shall have him whipped, as a warning. Then I shall let him go.'

But now crowds had gathered to hear what Pilate was going to say. Jesus' enemies had done their work well: this was an angry crowd. 'Kill him! Crucify him!' they cried.

Pilate was not a good ruler. He was afraid that the shouting would become a riot. So he handed Jesus over to be crucified.

Soldiers took Jesus' clothes. They mocked him, dressing him in a purple robe and crushing a crown of twisted thorns on his head. Then they beat him, thrust the heavy wooden cross onto his shoulders, and forced him to march to the place where he was to die.

There, on a hill outside the city, Jesus was nailed to a rough wooden cross and left to die. Two criminals were crucified that same day, one on either side.

As Jesus hung dying the sky went dark.

12 A Green Hill

Jesus' friends watched from a distance as Jesus died on the cross. At the end of the day Joseph from Arimathea went to Pilate. 'Please let me take the body,' he asked. 'I will arrange to bury it.'

Joseph and a small group of friends took the body, and laid it in a tomb. By now the sun was setting. Soon it would be the Sabbath—the day that God's laws said must be a day of rest.

Hurriedly, the friends rolled the stone door across the tomb. They could return later to prepare the body properly for the burial. Now they must go.

The stories of Jesus say that he was crucified on a hilltop just outside Jerusalem.

This Easter garden is a traditional way of remembering what happened on that terrible Good Friday. There are three crosses for the three who were crucified. Below is a tomb with a round stone door.

Easter garden

You will need

soil and grass seed

large garden tray

small flowerpot

scissors

old tights or thin, stretchy fabric

watering-can

small twigs and raffia

greenery

a large, flat stone

1 Mix the soil with the grass seed.

2 Take a large garden tray and half fill it with some of the soil. Put the flowerpot on its side roughly in the middle of the tray.

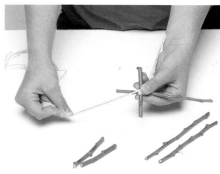

3 Cut a large piece from old tights or similar stretchy fabric and knot it into a bag. Fill this with more soil. Arrange it in a hump over the flowerpot, to create a 'hill' with a 'cave' at the bottom.

4 Water the soil thoroughly. Keep the soil moist and let the grass grow. It will take 3–4 weeks. Trim the grass a little as it appears, so it does not get too long.

5 Cut short pieces of twig and tie them with raffia to make little crosses. Arrange three crosses in the soil on the hilltop. Arrange other greenery around your garden. Put the stone by the entrance to the 'cave'.

Easter Sunday

Good Friday is a time of sadness. But the story of Jesus is not over. By Easter Sunday, people are telling amazing news.

The Sabbath day of rest passed. Early on Sunday morning, while it was still dark, a small group of women went to Jesus' tomb. They brought with them spices, for it was the tradition to wrap spices among the bandages that were wound round the body left in the tomb.

Suddenly, they gasped. There was the tomb, but the stone door was open. They went into the low cave, but the body of Jesus was not there.

Then they saw something: two figures dressed in shining white. The women fell to the ground, trembling. Then the two spoke: 'Why are you looking among the dead for one who is alive?' they asked. 'Jesus is not here; he is risen.'

The women went and told their story to the other friends of Jesus.

'But that's ridiculous,' they sneered. 'It's impossible! There must be some other explanation. We saw Jesus dead.'

One of the women, Mary Magdalene, was in the garden as the dawn came. She was weeping. Where was the body of her dear friend Jesus? She simply did not know.

A man came and stood by her. 'Why are you crying?' he asked. 'Who are you looking for?'

Mary looked round. In the half-light, she did not see clearly who was there, but she thought it must be the person who looked after the garden of olive trees. Perhaps he knew what had happened.

'O sir, tell me where you have put him and I will go and get him,' she sobbed.

The man spoke again: 'Mary.'

She turned and looked. It was Jesus.

On Easter Sunday, it is traditional for Christians to add flowers to their Easter garden—a reminder of the new life of spring, and of the new life they believe God gave Jesus.

You can add flowers by making small posies. Wrap the stems in damp tissue paper and cover this with kitchen foil. Make holes in the garden with a pencil, and push the posies into place.

14 Trees at Easter

In winter, many trees have bare branches. At Eastertime, new leaves are opening up. Some trees are covered in pink or white blossom.

For those who know the story of Jesus, it is a reminder of the Easter message: death is not the end. There is new life, new hope.

Enjoy watching the world come alive in spring. Make an indoor tree to help mark the festival.

Twig tree

You will need

bare branches

flowerpot

soil

pebbles

pencil

green card

scissors

cutting mat

a wooden skewer

masking tape

1 First collect some bare branches—perhaps twigs that have been pruned in winter. Put them in a pot of soil. Put stones on top to hold them firmly.

2 Draw leaf shapes on green card like the ones shown below. Cut them out.

3 Resting on the cutting mat, draw a line with a wooden skewer to mark the centre vein on each leaf. Fold each leaf along this line.

4 Unfold each leaf and tape it to the twigs. Find out how to make some springtime decorations for the tree on the next page.

15 Flowers and Birds

You will need

pencil

thin card

scissors

coloured paper

needle

silver thread

clear sticky tape

Flowers:

coloured beads

1 Copy the shape shown at the back of this book onto thin card and cut it out. You can now use it to draw round on the coloured paper to make flower shapes. Cut these out.

2 Now make the bead loop. Choose one bead to hang in the centre. This is the one you will see most. Then choose beads to go on each side. Choose 6–8 beads for each side.

3 Thread the needle with 40 cm of silver thread. Pick up the beads one at a time, starting with the beads for one side, then the centre bead, and then the other side. Hold the thread at both ends so the beads swing to the centre.

4 Knot the beads into a loop, as shown. Knot the thread about 2 cm further up. Tape the bead tassel on the paper flower shape at the top point.

5 Curl the card round the tassel and shape into a bellflower. Tape in place on the inside. Tie the ends of the thread into a loop and hang the bellflower on the tree.

Birds:

wooden skewer

ruler

coloured pencils

glue

feathers

1 Copy the bird shape shown at the back of this book on to thin card and cut it out. Draw round it on the coloured paper and cut that out. Then use a wooden skewer against a ruler to score a line from beak tip to tail tip.

2 Copy the wing shape at the back of this book on to thin card and cut it out. Draw round it on a folded piece of coloured paper. Cut the shape through both thicknesses so you have a pair of wings.

3 Draw the eyes on the bird shape and colour the beak on both sides.

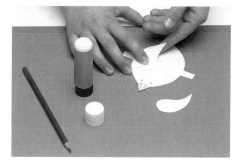

4 Spread some glue on the wrong side of the wing shapes in the area marked on the template and stick these in place.

5 Fold the bird in half along the line you scored and snip a tiny V away from the tail tip, as shown.

6 Unfold the bird and tape a feather in place as a tail. Make a stitch of silver thread at the points shown on the template and leave the ends dangling on the inside.

7 Fold the bird along the line again, and fold the tabs at the bottom inwards so they overlap. Tape them together. Knot the thread ends to make a hanging loop.

Spring bursts today,
For Christ is risen and all the earth's
    at play.

Flash forth, thou Sun,
The rain is over and gone, its work
    is done.

Winter is past,
Sweet Spring is come at last, is come
    at last.

Sing, Creatures, sing,
Angels and Men and Birds and
    everything.

Christina Rossetti
Selected verse

As surely as seeds sprout and grow,
the God who is Lord of all the world
will put right every wrong.

From the book of Isaiah, in the Bible

God's promise of resurrection
is written not only in books
but in every springtime leaf.

Martin Luther

17 Easter Nest

Eggs are part of the traditional Easter celebrations. For Christians, they are another reminder of new life.

Make a little nest of eggs for Easter.

You will need

75 g butter

2 tbsp golden syrup

150 g chocolate

150 g puffed rice cereal

a few chocolate 'twigs'

marzipan or foil-wrapped chocolate eggs

bowl

wooden spoon

paper cake cases

teaspoon

☺ *Ask a grown-up to help you cook.*

☺ *Always wash your hands before you begin.*

1 Put the butter, syrup and chocolate in a bowl. Microwave in 30-second bursts until the butter melts.

2 Add the cereal and stir the mixture.

3 Spoon the chocolate mixture into the cases.

4 Shape the 'nests' with a teaspoon.

5 Push in pieces of chocolate twig. Leave to set.

6 Wash your hands. Then shape the marzipan eggs. Place the eggs in the nests.

In springtime, many animals have babies. The whole world seems to come to life!

Make some Easter baby bunny biscuits:

You will need

150 g flour

50 g caster sugar

100 g butter

writing icing

chocolate buttons and other decorations

bowl

knife

rolling-pin

pastry cutters (or pencil, card and knife)

greased baking tray

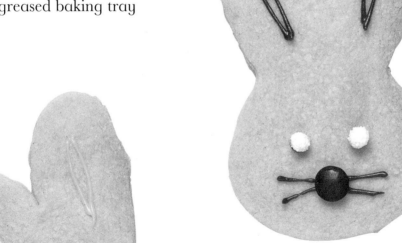

☺ *Ask a grown-up to help you cook.*

☺ *Always wash your hands before you begin.*

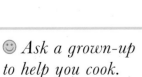

1 Put the flour and sugar into a bowl. Cut the butter into cubes and tip them in.

2 Break the butter into pieces and, with your fingertips, rub it into the flour until the mixture looks like fine breadcrumbs.

3 Squeeze the mixture into a lump.

4 Place on a clean surface and roll out.

5 Cut shapes with pastry cutters. If you can't get any the right shape, simply draw the shape you want onto card. Lay this on the rolled out biscuit mix and cut round it with a knife. Place the biscuits on the tray and bake for 10–12 minutes at 160°C.

6 Ask a grown-up to lift the biscuits out of the oven. After a few minutes, they will be hard enough to lift onto a rack to cool. When they are cool, add faces using the ideas shown. Make a little blob of icing to glue the chocolate decorations in place.

19 Easter Basket

A basket filled with gifts is an Easter tradition many people enjoy. Here is a basket you can make. Fill it with cookies or eggs for a wonderful gift.

You will need

metal ruler

thick white card (or heavy watercolour board)

pencil

cutting board

craft knife

wooden skewer

acrylic paints

old plate

thick paintbrushes

holepunch

scissors

ribbons

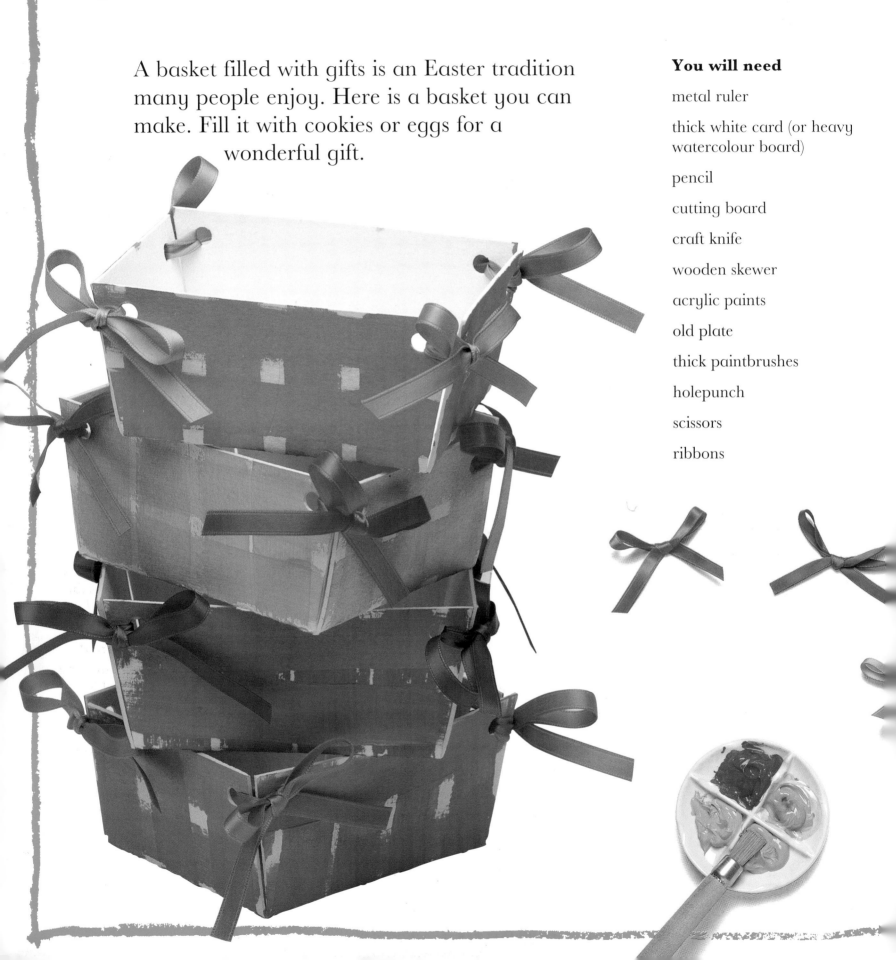

1 Use the template at the back of this book and copy it onto the card, using a ruler and a pencil. Ask a grown-up to help you cut it out on the cutting mat using a craft knife held against a metal ruler.

2 Use a wooden skewer held against the ruler to mark the fold lines. Then fold the card up, using a ruler along the groove to help keep the fold straight.

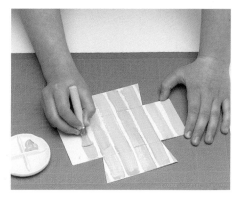

3 Paint your box. Put some paint on an old plate. Dip your brush in the paint and make long brush strokes in one direction, leaving a little gap between each line of paint. Leave to dry.

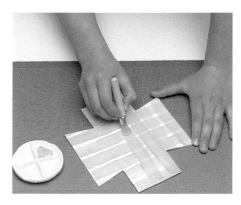

4 Now make brush strokes in the opposite direction. Leave a gap between each so you make a square pattern as shown. Leave to dry.

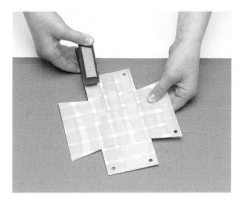

5 Use a holepunch to make holes as shown on the shape.

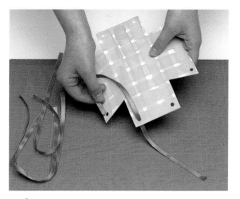

6 Cut the ribbon into four 50-cm lengths. Pull two corners of the box together. Working from the outside, first push the right-hand end of the ribbon into the right-hand hole, and the left-hand end of the ribbon into the left-hand hole. Pull it tight. Now take the left-hand end and thread it from the inside through the right-hand hole. Take the right-hand end out through the left-hand hole. Tie the ends in a bow on the outside. Do the same for all four corners.

It's great to have a card from someone who loves you. Make some cards to give to people you love this Easter.

You will need

coloured card

scissors

metal ruler

pencil

wooden skewer

stickers

glue

cutting mat

craft knife

ribbon

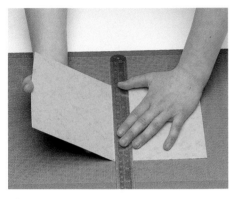

1 Ask a grown-up to help cut a rectangle of card, twice the size of the finished card you want to make. Measure halfway across top and bottom. Using a ruler and a wooden skewer, mark a crease. Fold along the crease, using a ruler to help keep the fold straight.

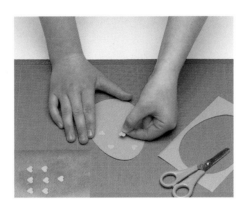

2 Draw an Easter egg shape on a different colour card and cut it out. Make it bright with stickers!

3 Glue the egg shape to the folded card. Mark a line each side of the egg where you want the ribbon to be. Now unfold the card on the cutting mat and ask a grown-up to help you cut slits along these lines, using the craft knife against the ruler.

4 Cut 50 cm ribbon and thread an end through each slit from the inside of the card. Use the end of the skewer to help push it through.

5 Centre the ribbon over the egg and tie in a bow. Trim the ends of the ribbon if they have got a bit raggy.

**template for bird
on page 15**

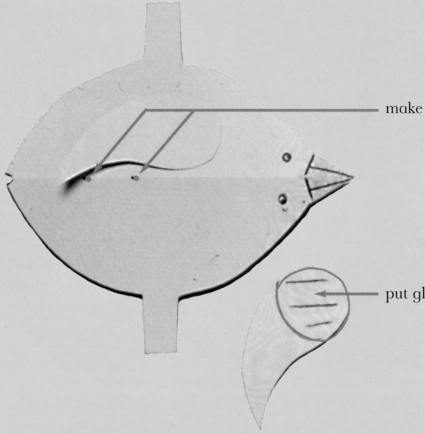

make holes for sewing

put glue on this part of the wing

how to stick the beads in place

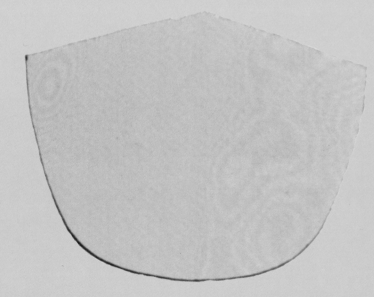

template for flower on page 15

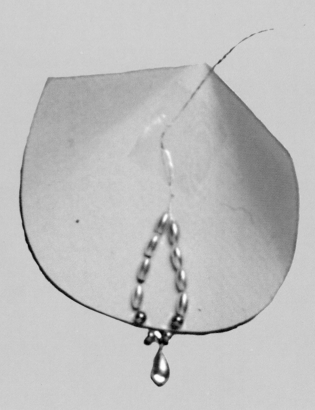

template for Easter basket on page 19

Other titles from Lion Children's Books

First Festivals: Christmas   *Lois Rock*

Look What I Made!   *Christina Goodings*

The Easter Story   *Lois Rock and Diana Mayo*

The Story of the Cross   *Mary Joslin and Gail Newey*